NOW YOU CAN READ ABOUT...
ANIMALS

TEXT BY STEPHEN ATTMORE
AND HARRY STANTON

BRIMAX BOOKS • NEWMARKET • ENGLAND

Illustrations by:

Eric Rowe

R. Hersey

J. Francis

G. Allen

T. Hayward

E. Turner

P. Weare

C. Newman

J. Rignall

The texts and illustrations in this book
have been published as separate volumes
by Brimax Books.
© BRIMAX RIGHTS LTD 1984. All rights reserved
Published by BRIMAX BOOKS, Newmarket, England 1984
ISBN 0 86112 261 5
Second printing 1985
Printed in Hungary

CONTENTS

DOGS

Here is a dog. His name is Patch.

He is a friendly dog.

Look at Patch's big, floppy ears.

He can hear Sam and Tina coming.

His tail wags. He is happy.

Sam and Tina look after Patch.

Patch likes it when they come.

He is lonely on his own all day.

Patch is not a big dog.

But he is not a small dog.

Can you see Patch's claws?

How many claws are on each paw?

Patch has got lots of teeth.

There are six big ones at the top

and six big ones at the bottom.

Patch is a father. Here are the
three puppies. They are with
their mother. All puppies are
born blind and deaf. They are
now twelve days old. Their eyes
are open and they can hear.
They have a few teeth, but not
as many as Patch or their mother.

Their mother washes, grooms and feeds the puppies.

Patch looks after the puppies and their mother. He barks when people or other animals come too close.

Would you like a puppy for a pet?
It must be six weeks old before
it can leave its parents. Do not
play with the puppy all day.
A puppy needs plenty of sleep.
Remember to feed your puppy
every day.

Puppies need love and care. They
get lonely if they have no one
to play with. A puppy with short
hair must have its coat brushed
once or twice a week. A puppy
with long hair must be brushed
every day. Patch has a bath every
four weeks.

Have you seen an angry dog? Patch is angry. His body is stiff. His hair is on end. He growls.

This puppy is playful. It is asking for a game. Its tail is wagging.

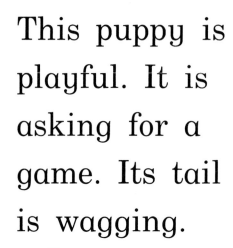

This dog is on guard. It is ready to attack. It is barking.

This dog is afraid. Its tail is between its legs. Its ears are back.

Sam is training Patch. He presses the dog's back and says, "Sit". If Patch sits, Sam gives him a pat on the back. Can you see Patch's collar? His name is on the collar.

There are many types of dogs.
These ones are called running
dogs. Look at their long legs.
They can run very fast.

A greyhound is a
running dog. Look
at its thin body.
Its tail is long.
Its ears are
folded back.
Greyhounds can
run very very
fast. Racing
greyhounds is
a sport in
some countries.

These dogs often work on farms.
They help the farmer to look
after the sheep and cattle. Look
for the very hairy dog. This is
an Old English sheepdog. How does
he see where he is going?

The dogs here pull sledges
over snow and ice. They are
strong dogs. They have thick hair
to help them keep warm. Look
at the dog with white hair.
He can hide in the snow.

The dogs here are gun dogs. They help hunters. Some of them chase animals. Other gun dogs sit by the person with the gun. When a bird or animal is shot, they run off to fetch it. They bring the animal back to the hunter.

These dogs have a good sense
of smell. They use their noses
to follow the scent of people or
animals. The biggest dog here is
a bloodhound. The police use
bloodhounds to track robbers.
Have these dogs got big noses?
No, but they have big ears.

Look at these big dogs. They are
guard dogs. What do you think
they guard? Do they look fierce?
These dogs come from many parts
of the world.

This is a labrador.
It is a guide dog.
Its owner is blind.
Look at the dog's
special lead. The
blind person is
holding the
handle. The guide
dog is taking
its owner safely
across the street.

These dogs are not kept as pets.
They are wild dogs.

The wolf is also
a very fast
runner. Look at
its long legs.

This wild dog
lives in
Australia. It is
called a dingo.

The fox is a
smaller wild dog.
Often it comes
out at night. It
is clever. It
keeps out of
sight. Look at
these two foxes.
They both have
very long, bushy
tails.

In this book you have met Patch
and his puppies. You have also
seen many other dogs.
Look for these dogs
when you go out.

Afghan hound   German Shepherd dog   Corgi

Saint Bernard   Poodle   Dalmatian

Beagle

Pekinese

This is the smallest dog. It is called a chihuahua (chi-wa-wa).

The largest dog is the mastiff.

CATS

Here is a cat. Her name is Bonny.
People love to stroke her fur.
Look at her slim body. She can
squeeze through holes in fences.
She can walk along narrow ledges.
Can you see Bonny's paws?
Her sharp claws help her grip.
Bonny has a rough tongue.
She uses this to lick up
food and to keep her coat clean.

Look at Bonny's eyes. Can you see
the dark slit in the middle?
At night, the dark part gets
larger. This helps her to see
in the dark. She can also feel
with her whiskers. This helps
her to find her way.

Bonny is a mother. She has
four kittens in her litter.
All kittens are born blind and
deaf. They are now ten days old.
Their eyes are open and they can
hear. They have a few teeth,
but not many. More fur has grown
on their bodies.

Bonny cleans,
washes and feeds
her kittens.

After a few weeks,
the kittens will
learn to lap milk
from a saucer.

Bonny carries her
kittens gently
in her mouth. She
brings them back
when they wander
too far. You must
not carry kittens
like this. You
might hurt them.

Kittens love to
play games. It is
fun. They pounce
on toy mice.
They pat balls.

Would you like a kitten for a pet? It must be ten weeks old before you can take it away from its mother. Kittens need love and care. You must feed and play with them.

A kitten will need to use a litter tray. Later it can be trained to go outside.

When it is older,
you should brush
and comb your
kitten each day.
This is in case
it picks up fleas.

Your kitten will
sleep happily on
a soft blanket in
a box or basket.
It may miss its
mother at first.

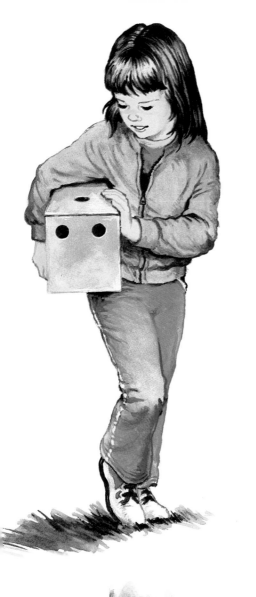

Think of a name
for your kitten.

A box like this
is useful. You
could use it when
you take your
kitten to a vet.
The vet will help
you to look after
your kitten.

Your kitten needs
a post on which
to sharpen its
claws.

Have you seen
an angry cat?
Bonny is angry.
Her back arches
and her fur
stands on end.
She is trying
to look bigger.
Her claws are out.
She is ready
to fight.

Her kitten has
run away. He is
afraid of the
dog. Can you see
him in the tree?

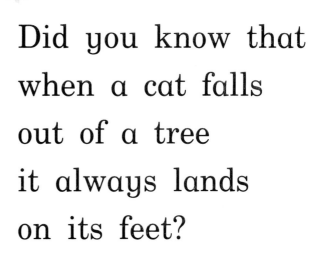

Did you know that
when a cat falls
out of a tree
it always lands
on its feet?

Cats make many noises. They purr
when they are happy. They hiss
when they are angry. They miaow
when they want you to take notice.

There are many types of cats.
These cats have short hair.
What colour is each cat?

Short hair cats
make great pets.
Their fine fur is
easy to comb.

Many cats have
more than one
colour in their
fur. This cat is
black and white.

Bonny's fur has
three colours.

43

These cats have long fur. Their
legs are short and their tails
are fluffy. Their long fur needs
looking after. The hairs get
tangled. Look at their noses.
Some of them have flat noses.

Some cats with long white fur
have orange eyes. Some have
blue eyes. Others have one blue
and one orange eye. That is odd!
White hair cats with blue eyes
are often deaf. That is sad!

This is a Burmese tom cat. He has yellow eyes. Look at his small paws. His tail is long and thin.

Siamese kittens are born white. They have blue eyes. This adult she cat has two colours. Can you see the other colour?

Look at this cat.
It is a manx cat.
What is missing?

This cat is a
chinchilla. The
tip of each hair
is black. This
makes the fur look
silver. His coat is
shining.

Some pet cats are
not looked after.
They run away.
They may become
wild cats.

Lions, tigers, cheetahs and
leopards all belong to the cat
family. They are much bigger
than Bonny. Most of the big cats
live in the wild. They hunt for
their food. The biggest cat is
the tiger. His dark stripes help
him hide in long grass.

Here is a lion. What a big cat!
The cheetah runs very fast.
A leopard can climb trees. They
jump down on to other animals.

There are not many big cats left.
Some of them live in safari parks
or zoos. You can see them there.

In this book you have met Bonny and her kittens. You have also seen some of the big wild cats.

You may see some of these cats when you go out.

One colour   Spotted   Tabby

Two colours   Three colours   Colour tipped

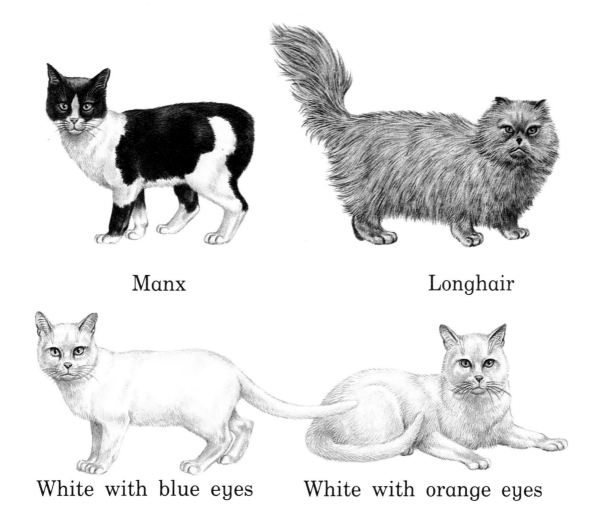

Manx

Longhair

White with blue eyes

White with orange eyes

Would you have
one of these
cats for a pet?

Bobcat

Lynx

Puma

HORSES and PONIES

Here is a pony. His name is Ross.
He is a happy pony. Boys
and girls love to ride on Ross.
Look at the long hair on his neck.
This is called his mane. Ross has
a long tail too, but his legs
are short. Can you see the pony's
hooves? These are his feet.

Ross is not a big pony. He is
a Welsh mountain pony. A pony is
a small horse. Ross is four years
old. We can tell the age of
a pony or a horse by its teeth.
Large adult teeth start growing
when the horse or pony is three.

Ross is a father.
Here is his son.
His name is Tiny.

Baby ponies or
baby horses are
called foals.
Tiny is only two
days old. He is
still wobbly on
his feet.

Tiny is being licked by his mother. She feeds him until he is about six months old. Tiny will be a foal until his first birthday. Then he will be a pony.

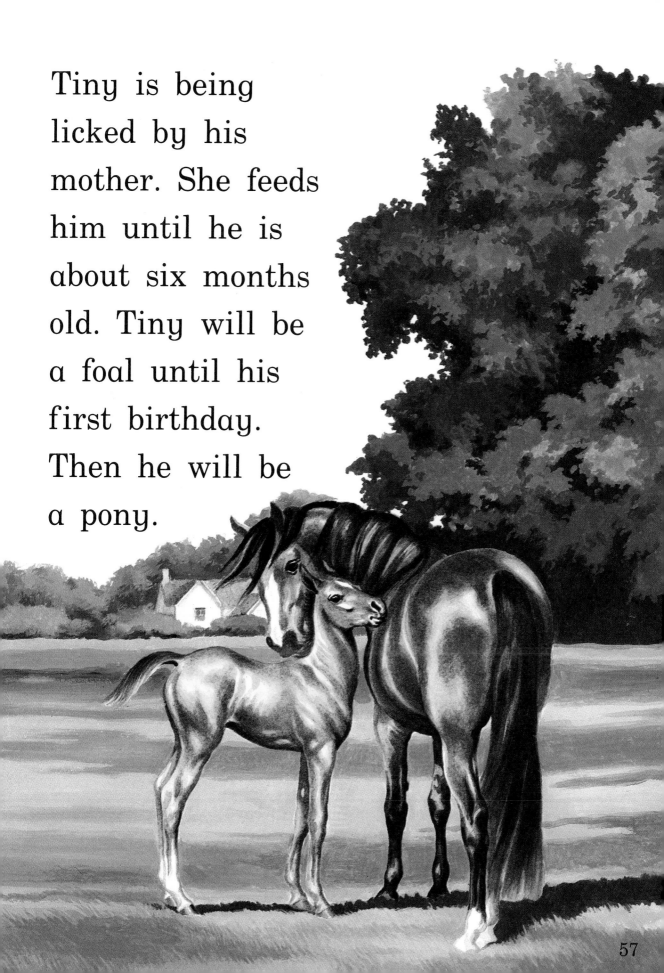

This girl is measuring Ross. How tall do you think he is? He is 11 hands tall. One 'hand' is equal to 10 centimetres. Look at the stick the girl is using. She is measuring from the ground to the top of his shoulder. This is how horses and ponies are measured.

This is the tallest horse in the world. It is called a Shire horse. It is very strong.

All ponies are smaller than 14 hands. The Shetland pony is only nine hands high.

Horses and ponies need love and
care. If they are ill you must
call a vet. Ross is kept in
a stable in winter. His stable
is cleaned out each day.
New straw is spread over the
floor. Ross drinks water and
eats hay and bran. He is brushed
and taken for a walk every day.

Did you know that horses and ponies wear shoes? They have metal shoes to protect their feet. Look at the blacksmith fitting new shoes. He has cut the horse's hooves. We cut our toenails when they grow too long. Horses and ponies have their hooves cut every six weeks.

Have you ever watched a horse moving? Look at this white horse. It is walking. It lifts its feet in turn. Its tail is lying down.

Now the horse is trotting. It is moving its legs in pairs. One front leg and one back leg are on the ground at the same time.

The horse is now going faster. It is running. We call this cantering. Look at its tail. It is swishing about.

The horse is running very fast. We call this galloping. Both of its back legs are off the ground at the same time.

Riding is fun. It is not easy.
You need to learn to ride. Look
at the boy sitting on the pony.
He has learnt to sit in the
saddle and hold the reins. His
teacher is leading the pony.

There is a lot to learn before a rider can begin to jump. Look at this girl riding Ross. They are jumping a small fence.

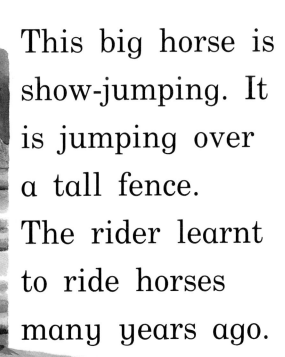

This big horse is show-jumping. It is jumping over a tall fence. The rider learnt to ride horses many years ago.

These horses are racing against each other. The men and women who ride them are called jockeys.

These people are riding horses in a game of polo. They try to hit the ball with their sticks.

Horses are used
for work. This is
a policeman riding
a horse.

Horses are used
to round-up
cattle and sheep
in some countries.
They work hard.

Have you ever
been to a circus?
This is a circus
horse.

A long time ago horses pulled coaches. They took people from place to place. Then they began to use motor cars instead. Have you seen horses pulling a coach?

Look at the pony pulling a cart.

Look at these big horses. They
are very strong. Some horses
still work in the fields. The
horses are helping the farmer.

Donkeys, mules and zebras
all belong to the horse family.

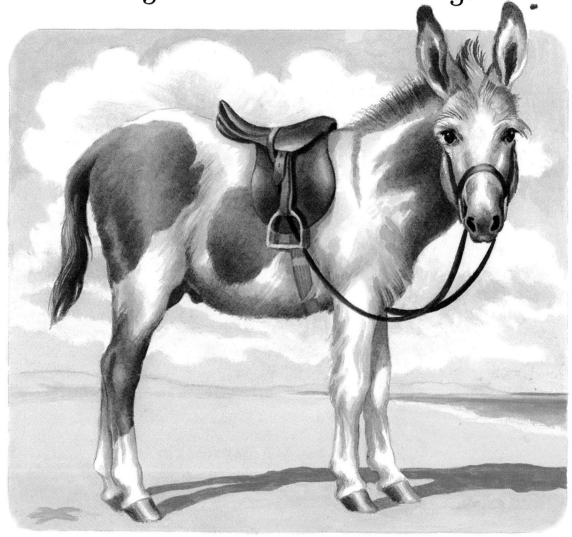

This is a donkey. Look at its big
ears. Have you ever seen donkeys
at the seaside? Boys and girls
ride up and down the beach
on them.

This is a mule.
It looks a bit
like a donkey.
It is bigger and
stronger than
Ross.

A zebra is easy
to spot. It has
black and white
stripes over its
body. It has ears
like a donkey.

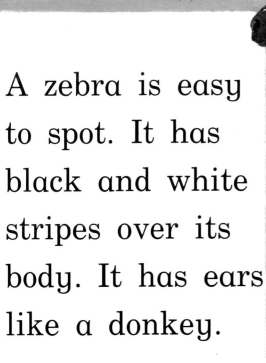

In this book you have met Ross. You have seen animals in the horse family. Look for some of them when you go out.

Piebald

Grey

Chestnut

Brown

Black

Markings

Star   Stripe   Snip   Blaze

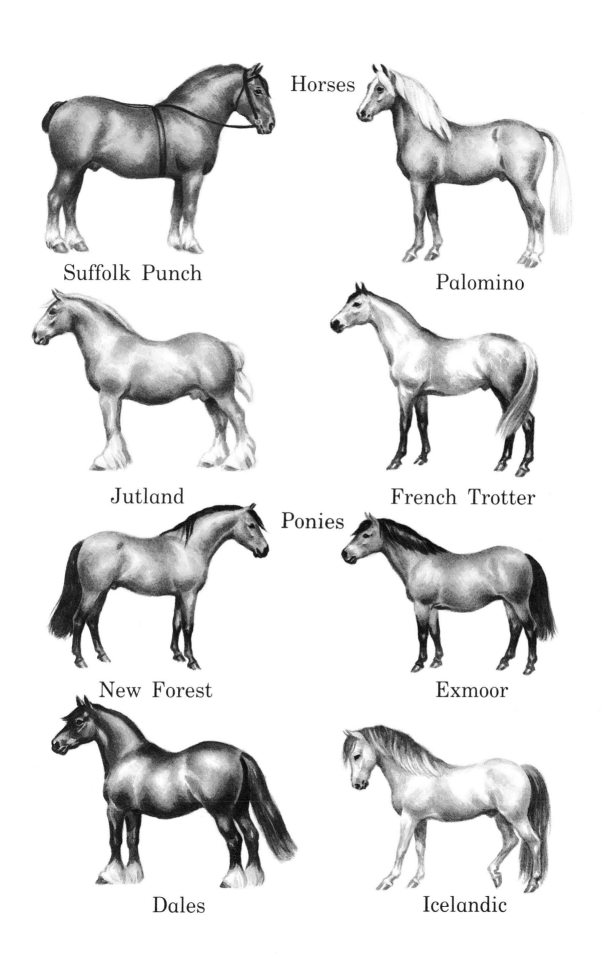

Horses

Suffolk Punch

Palomino

Jutland

French Trotter

Ponies

New Forest

Exmoor

Dales

Icelandic

PETS

Here is a pet store. There are
lots of young animals. No one has
given them names. Can you think
of a name for each one? All the
pets in this shop are for sale.
Would you like one?

Look at the fluffy rabbits.
They are cuddly. Look at the
puppies. They look friendly.
There are so many pets. It is hard
to choose one you like best.
The goldfish is looking at you.

Mary wants a baby
rabbit as a pet.
It is a little
ball of fluff.
It sits in Mary's
hands. Mary calls
it Fluffy.

But Fluffy will
grow—and GROW
—and GROW.
Then it will be
a very big ball
of fluff.

Tom is in the pet store. He sees a baby goldfish in a big tank. It is pretty. He buys the baby goldfish to take home.

He calls his new pet Goldie. Tom carries Goldie home. He is very careful. He must not spill Goldie.

All pets need to be looked after.
Some pets like you to cuddle and
stroke them. Mary is picking up
Fluffy. She has one hand on the
neck to steady the rabbit. Look at
the furry pet in the box. This is
a guinea pig. The kitten is
playing a game. It is fun.

Some pets must not be cuddled.
They are afraid. Look at the little
bird in the cage. It is a canary.
The boy must be careful. The canary
might fly away. Tom uses a net
to pick up his pet goldfish.
Goldie must not be out of water
for long or he will die.

Tom is taking Goldie to its new home. His father has made a pond behind the house for goldfish. Now Tom can buy more goldfish. Goldie will have some friends in the pond.

Fluffy lives in a rabbit hutch.
It has two rooms. One room has
wire mesh over the front. Fluffy
likes to look out of her hutch.
She sleeps in the other room
where it is warmer.

What is Fluffy eating? You must give your pet the right food. Ask the people at the pet store. They will tell you what food to give your pet.

This puppy is eating meat. The kitten is lapping milk. You must give your pet fresh food and water every day.

Look at the mice
in their cage.
They have their
food in a little
dish. The bottle
is full of water.
The mice suck
water through the
tube at the
bottom.

Tom is putting
fish food on the
pond for Goldie.
Look at the ring.
This stops the
food spreading.

Mary is cleaning out the hutch.
She is taking out all the straw.
Then she will put in fresh straw.
Fluffy is in a pen. She is
running and hopping. Mary's friend
Anna is brushing her guinea pig.
This guinea pig has long hair.
Anna brushes it every day.

This is a hamster. Its cage
is cleaned out every few days.
If it is not cleaned out, there
is a nasty smell. Look at
the hamster. It is holding food
in its paws. The hamster stores
some food in its cheeks. That is
why its face looks fat.

It is cruel to keep a pet in
a cage for a long time. Pets
need to run around. Look at the
hamster and guinea pig. They are
in a play pen. It is indoors.

Look at the mouse
running inside
the wheel. The
other mouse is
running up the
plank.

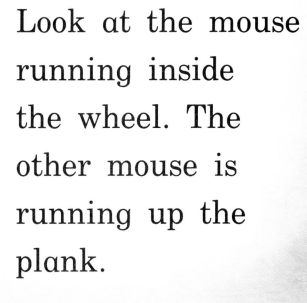

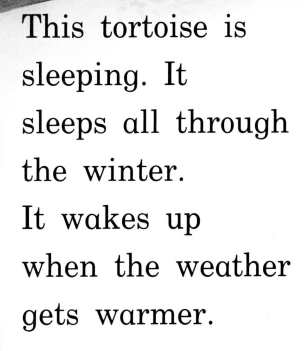

This tortoise is
sleeping. It
sleeps all through
the winter.
It wakes up
when the weather
gets warmer.

Fluffy has a log in her cage.
She bites the bark with her big
front teeth. This stops the teeth
from growing too long. If they
do grow too long, Fluffy will not
be able to eat.

Many pets have claws. Their claws
may grow too long. Look at the vet
cutting the hamster's claws. A vet
will help you look after your pet.

Here are some other animals.
Would you like one of these
for a pet?

Look for the
insect on the
plant. Can you
find it? It is
a stick insect.

This is a frog.
He lives in the
pond. Tom likes
to watch the
tadpoles change
into frogs.

This is a talking
bird. It is
a parrot.

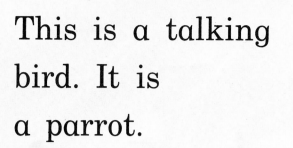

This is a small
monkey. It is
eating the leaves
in the tree. Can
you think of
a name for this
pet monkey?

This is a goat.
Look at his beard
and his horns.

In this book you have met Goldie the goldfish and Fluffy the rabbit. You have also seen other pets. Look out for these pets.

Goldfish   Dog   Cat   Pony

English rabbit   Rex rabbit   Dutch rabbit

Guinea pig   Hamster   Mouse

Tortoise   Frog   Gerbil

Parrot   Cockatoo   Canary

DINOSAURS

Dinosaur means terrible
lizard. They were the
largest animals to have
walked on the earth.
The largest dinosaurs
weighed up to fifty tonnes
and were about twenty five
metres long.

No one ever saw
a dinosaur.
Dinosaurs died
out long before
there were ever
any men or women
on the earth.

Each Brontosaurus dinosaur weighed as much as six elephants.
Brontosaurus stayed together in herds because they were attacked by meat eating dinosaurs.

Brontosaurus
(*Bron-toh-sawrus*)

The largest dinosaurs were the Diplodocus. They were as long as three railway coaches. They were able to raise their heads very high so that they could eat leaves from the tops of trees.

Diplodocus
(Dip-lod-oh-cus)

Some of them did not eat plants. These were the meat eating dinosaurs. They ate other dinosaurs.

Tyrannosaurus Rex
(Ty-ran-oh-sawrus Rex)

The Tyrannosaurus Rex were the largest of the meat eating dinosaurs. They stood on their back legs and were over six metres high. They weighed eight tonnes. Tyrannosaurus Rex had long sharp teeth and very short arms.

Many plant eating dinosaurs ran away when they were attacked. But some who were slow moving had armour.

Stegosaurus was as long as a bus. On its back it had two rows of bony plates for armour. There were no plates on its side to protect it.

Stegosaurus
(Steg-oh-sawrus)

Ankylosaurus
(An-kyle-oh-sawrus)

The flat back of the
Ankylosaurus was covered
in armour.

Look at the bony club at
the end of its tail. It
could use the club if it
had to fight other dinosaurs.

These strange bone-headed
dinosaurs had very thick
skulls. The bone of their
skulls was over twenty
five centimetres thick.
This protected them when
they fought.

Look at the long horn which the Parasaurolophus had on the back of their heads. They ate leaves with jaws that looked like a duck's beak. Inside their jaws they had hundreds of small sharp teeth. Unlike you and I when the teeth wore down they grew new ones.

Parasaurolophus
(Para-saw-roh-loh-fus)

Triceratops
(Try-sair-oh-tops)

The Triceratops had three very long horns. One on its nose and one over each eye. Covering its neck it had a shield of bone. Triceratops had flat teeth to help it eat tough leaves.

Another horned dinosaur was the
Styracosaurus. It had a horn on
its nose seventy centimetres long.
Its head was over two metres long
and it weighed three and a half
tonnes.

Styracosaurus
(Sty-rak-oh-sawrus)

Horned dinosaurs ate plants. With
their sharp horns they charged any
other dinosaurs that attacked them.

At the same time as the dinosaurs, strange creatures hunted in the sea. Ichthyosaurs means fish lizard. It had sharp teeth and large eyes.
Plesiosaurs were about twelve metres long. They had large flat flippers and very long necks.

Plesiosaurs
(Ples-e-oh-saws)

Ichthyosaurs
(Ik-thee-oh-saws)

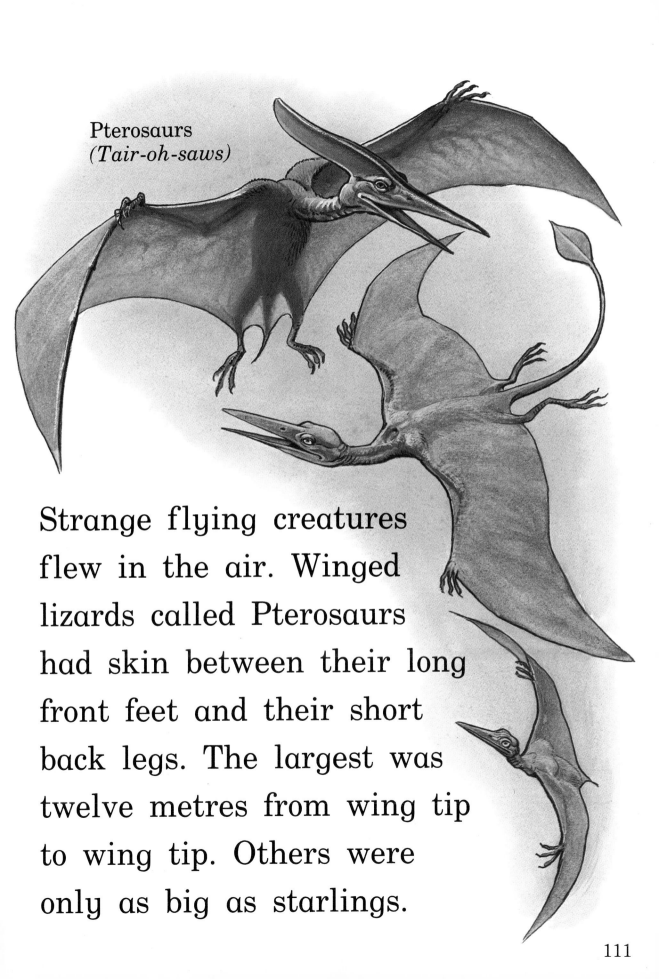

Pterosaurs
(Tair-oh-saws)

Strange flying creatures
flew in the air. Winged
lizards called Pterosaurs
had skin between their long
front feet and their short
back legs. The largest was
twelve metres from wing tip
to wing tip. Others were
only as big as starlings.

The age of dinosaurs came to an end.
All the dinosaurs died out when
the earth became cooler about
sixty five million years ago.
This did not happen suddenly. It
took thousands of years.

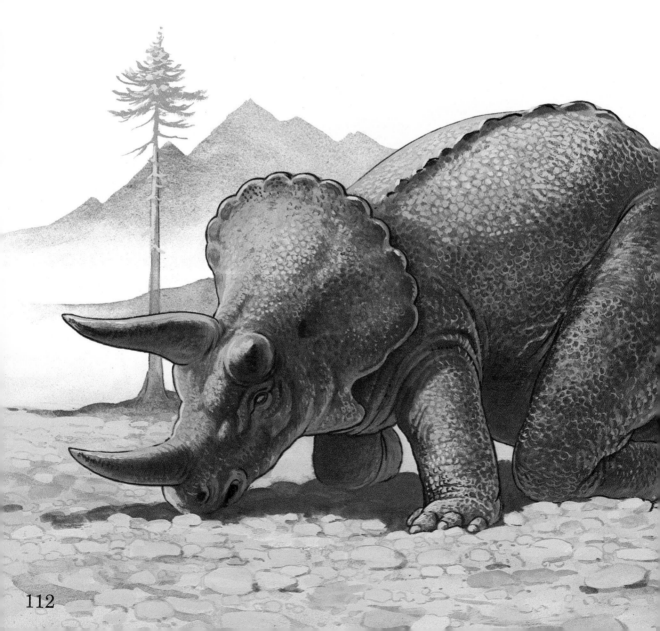

Perhaps it was too cold for them to live or perhaps their food did not grow.

Even the strange creatures that flew in the air and those that swam in the sea died out.

The bones of some dinosaurs can still be found today. When some of the creatures died they fell into soft mud. This mud gradually hardened. The bones then became fossils and the mud around them hardened into rock.

Some fossils are found when the rock is worn away. Other fossils are found in mines or stone quarries.

What are the names of these Dinosaurs?

Brontosaurus

Stegosaurus

Styracosaurus

Parasaurolophus

Pterosaurs

Tyrannosaurus Rex

Dipolodocus

Bone-headed Dinosaurs

Triceratops

Ankylosaurs

Plesiosaurs

Ichthyosaurs

WILD ANIMALS

Here are some big
wild animals. Look
at the giraffe.
What is it eating?
A giraffe can see
a long way. It is
the tallest animal
in the world.
What a long neck!
Zebras look like
striped horses.
They eat grass.
They can smell
other animals
a long way away.

The elephants are having a shower.
They suck up water in their trunks
and spray it over their backs.
An elephant's trunk is a very
long nose. Look at the baby
elephant standing between its
mother's legs.

The lion is the king of wild
animals. Lions live and hunt in a
group called a pride. They kill
and eat zebras and giraffes.
Lion cubs have dark spots on
their sides. Look at the cheetah
running. It is the fastest animal
on land. It can run at 70 mph.

These wild animals are hyenas.
They howl when they are excited.
The sound is like people laughing.
This is an anteater. Look at its
long snout. It pushes its long,
sticky tongue into ants' nests
and eats the ants.

The hippopotamus is a big animal.
Its name means 'river horse'.
Hippos stay in the water for most
of the day. This keeps them cool.
They come out onto the land at night
to eat grass. Look for the small
eyes on top of the hippo's head.

A rhinoceros is a heavy creature.
It eats leaves, twigs and grass.
In the evening, rhinos roll in
the mud beside a river. This helps
them to cool down. Look at the
two rhinos charging at each other.

These animals live in forests in
North America. Look at the beaver.
It uses its sharp teeth to chop
down small trees. Beavers build
dams across streams. The bear cub
is climbing a tree. The animal
with prickly spikes is a porcupine.

These animals live in woods in
Europe. The female deer is eating
twigs and buds. Look at the antlers
on the head of the male deer.
Each year they drop off and new
ones grow. Look for the baby deer.
The red foxes are stalking the
deer. Look at their bushy tails.

Some wild animals live in trees.
Look at the monkeys. They are
eating fruit and leaves. They leap
from tree to tree. Gorillas are
much larger. When they walk they
use their hands and their feet.
When a gorilla is angry it hoots.
It beats its chest with its hands.

Look at the squirrel. The long
bushy tail helps it to balance on
the branch. A squirrel's home is
called a drey. Look for the bats
hanging upside down. They sleep
during the day and fly at night.
They have thin skin between their
long fingers. This is like a wing.

These wild animals live in
Australia. Look for the baby
kangaroo. It is peeping out of
a pouch on its mother's tummy.
Look at the kangaroos leaping.
They have strong back legs.

Koalas live in trees. They feed at night on leaves and shoots. The baby koala is clinging to its mother's back. The duck-billed platypus lays eggs in a burrow. It has small ears and small eyes. Its bill is covered in skin and has nostrils at the end.

Animals need water and food.
There is very little water or
food in hot desert lands.
Few animals live there. Camels
travel long distances without
stopping. They store water in their
bodies. In a sandstorm they close
their nostrils and eyes.

This small cat lives in a desert.
Its feet have thick pads on the
bottom. This makes it easier for
the cat to move on sand. It rests
during the day and hunts at night.
The gazelle feeds on grass and
roots. It can go without water for
over a week. It runs very fast.

Some wild animals live in the
mountains. The puma is leaping
down on to a llama. Pumas are also
called cougars. A snow leopard is
following a yak. What long horns
the yak has!

Chipmunks live in long tunnels.
They carry food in their cheek
pouches. They store nuts, seeds,
fruit and berries to eat in
winter. Look at the mountain goat
on a high ledge. It feeds on grass.

Only a few animals live in the cold
lands near the North and South
poles. Look at the walruses.
What long tusks! Did you know that
walruses swim underwater on their
backs? They break through the ice
on the surface with their tusks.

This big white animal is a polar
bear. It kills and eats seals.
It has hairy soles on its feet.
These stop it from sliding on the
ice. Baby bears are born blind.
They stay in a den with their
mother until spring comes.

In this book you have read about many wild animals. Do you know where these wild animals live?

Buffalo

Tiger

Giant panda

Chimpanzee

Wombat

Camel

Ibex

Sea-lion

Musk ox

REPTILES

Crocodiles and lizards
are reptiles. So are
snakes and turtles.
A tortoise is also
a reptile—have you
got one as a pet?

There are over six thousand different kinds of reptiles. They can be very different in shape. Some of them live on land. Some of them live in water and some even live in trees.

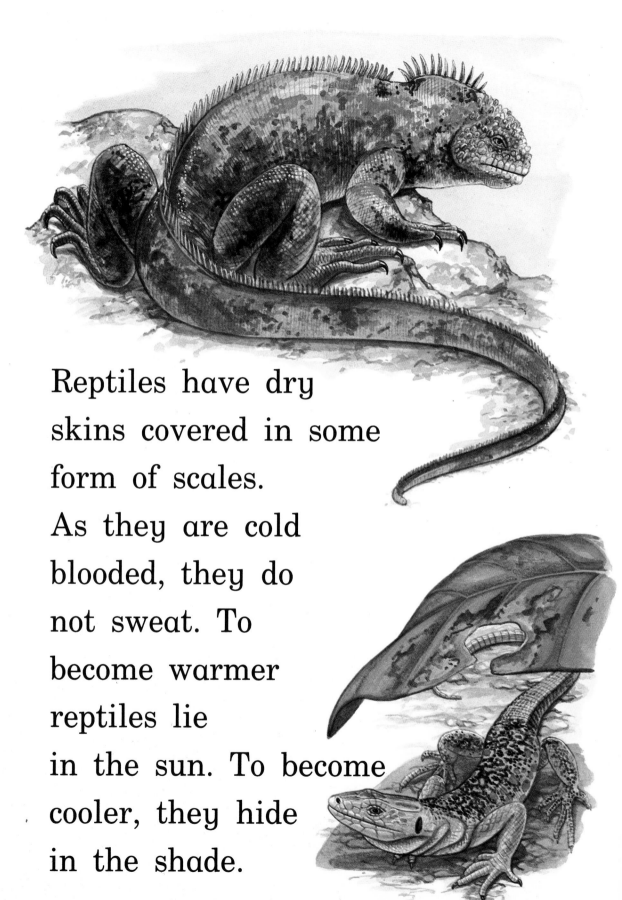

Reptiles have dry
skins covered in some
form of scales.
As they are cold
blooded, they do
not sweat. To
become warmer
reptiles lie
in the sun. To become
cooler, they hide
in the shade.

In the colder parts of the world
snakes, lizards and tortoises
may sleep during the winter.
They hide in a warm, dry
place until spring.

Crocodiles and alligators live
in warm rivers. They can
grow very big. Some are over
six metres long.

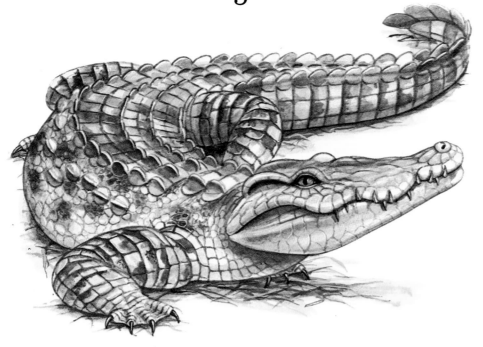

Crocodiles have heavy bodies
and short strong legs. They
can walk and even run on land.
With the help of a strong tail
and webbed feet, they are very
good swimmers.

Alligators and crocodiles
eat fish, snails and crabs
they find in the water.
Crocodiles lay up to sixty
eggs in a mud lined nest.
The mother guards the nest
until they hatch.
The babies have to find their
own food, but the mother will
guard them for a week or two.

They also lie in wait with only their eyes and noses above the water.
They are ready for any animals and birds that may come down to the water's edge for a drink.

There are over two hundred different kinds of tortoise.

Some of them live on land, some live in water. They move very slowly. They are able to hide from their enemies by pulling their head, legs and tail into their thick shells.

On the Galapagos Islands in the Pacific Ocean are the biggest and oldest tortoises in the world. The giant tortoise is so large that a man can ride on its back. The oldest is over one hundred and fifty years of age.

Sea Turtles live in the ocean. The males seldom go ashore. The females only go ashore to lay their eggs. They dig holes in sandy beaches, in which to lay their eggs.

The female covers the eggs with sand. The heat of the sun helps to hatch the eggs. Sixty days later baby turtles scramble down the beach to the sea.

Lizards can be found in all parts of the world. Some live in trees. Some live in deserts. Many of them burrow underground. A few can even glide from tree to tree.

The smallest lizards may only be a few centimetres long. Largest of all are the Komodo Dragons. These live on islands in the Pacific Ocean. They can grow to over three metres in length.

There are nearly three thousand different kinds of snakes. Very few of them are poisonous. Many are harmless. Some snakes kill their prey by coiling round it and squeezing hard. Others catch their prey in their jaws. They swallow it whole.

Here is a grass snake. Grass snakes like to live in damp places. They are good swimmers. They cannot harm you.

The cobra is a poisonous snake. This snake is found in Africa.

The anaconda is the largest snake in the world. It is as long as a bus or a coach. It kills its prey by squeezing it.

Rattlesnakes are found in America. They make a sound like a baby's rattle, to warn other creatures to keep away.

Swimming in the river is a red-bellied water snake.

Most chameleons live in trees. Their feet and tails can easily grip the branches. They move very little and hide by changing their colour.

To catch flies, a chameleon shoots out its long sticky tongue. This tongue may be almost as long as the chameleon.

Look at these pictures.
Do you know what these
reptiles are called?

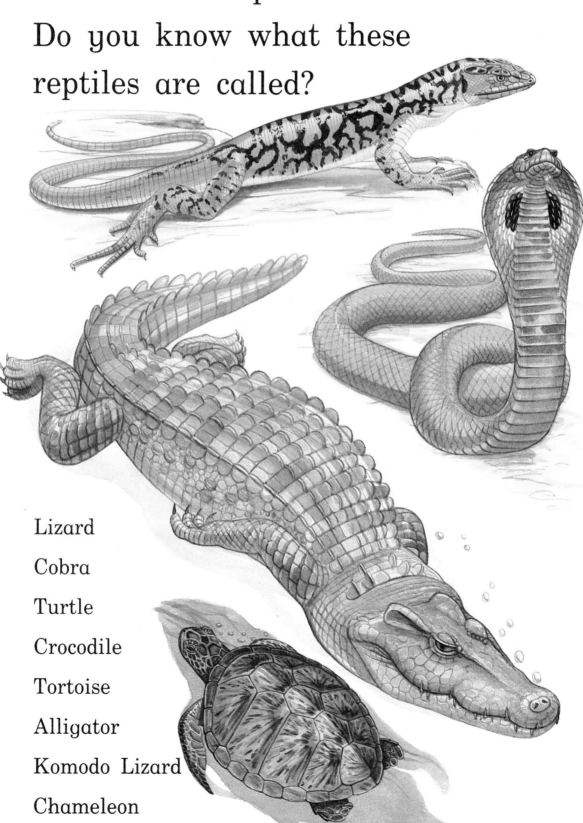

Lizard

Cobra

Turtle

Crocodile

Tortoise

Alligator

Komodo Lizard

Chameleon

Have you ever seen any
of these reptiles?

CREATURES
of the DEEP

This is a sailfish. It has a fin
like a sail on top of its body.
This fin stops the fish from
rolling over when it races through
the water. Sailfish can swim at
speeds of up to one hundred
kilometres an hour.

The swordfish
can also swim
very fast. It uses
its sword when
hunting smaller
fish.

There are many different
kinds of shark. The largest
is the whale shark. It is the
largest fish in the sea.
Whale sharks can only eat
very tiny creatures which
they find in the sea.

The great white
shark is very
dangerous. It has
powerful jaws and
rows of sharp
teeth. When a shark
loses a tooth it
grows another one.

Rays are flat
fish which seem
to fly through
the water.

Rays are very difficult to see.
They can change colour to match
the sea bed.

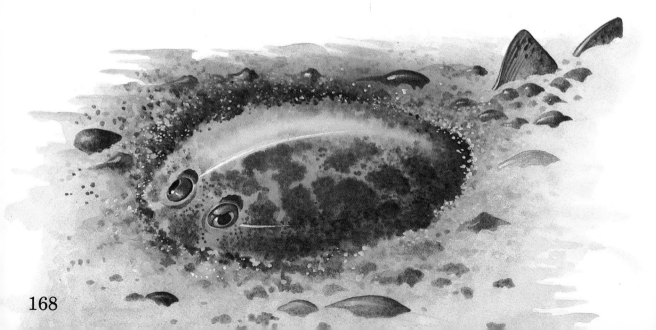

The electric ray
can catch its
prey by giving it
an electric shock.

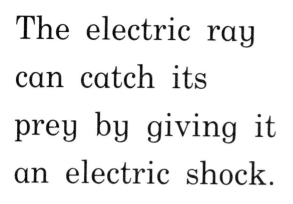

The sting ray
has a long whip-
like tail. With
this tail it stings
its enemies.

Whales are not fish. They are animals which live in the sea. They are not fish because they cannot breathe under water.

Blue whales are the largest creatures in the world. A fully grown blue whale weighs as much as fifteen elephants.

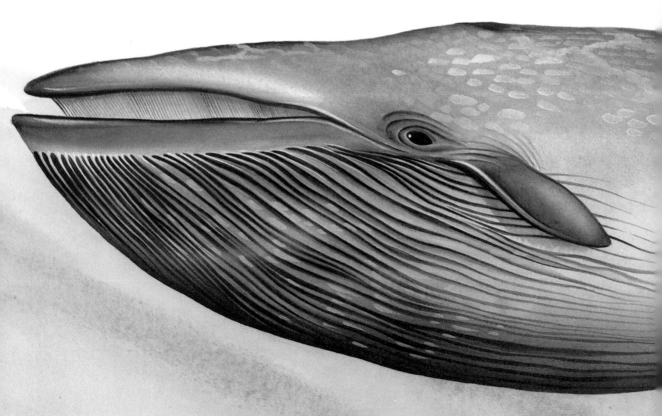

Dolphins often follow
ships as they sail
along. They race through
the water leaping
over the waves.

Eels are long
thin fish
found in
rivers, ponds
and the sea.

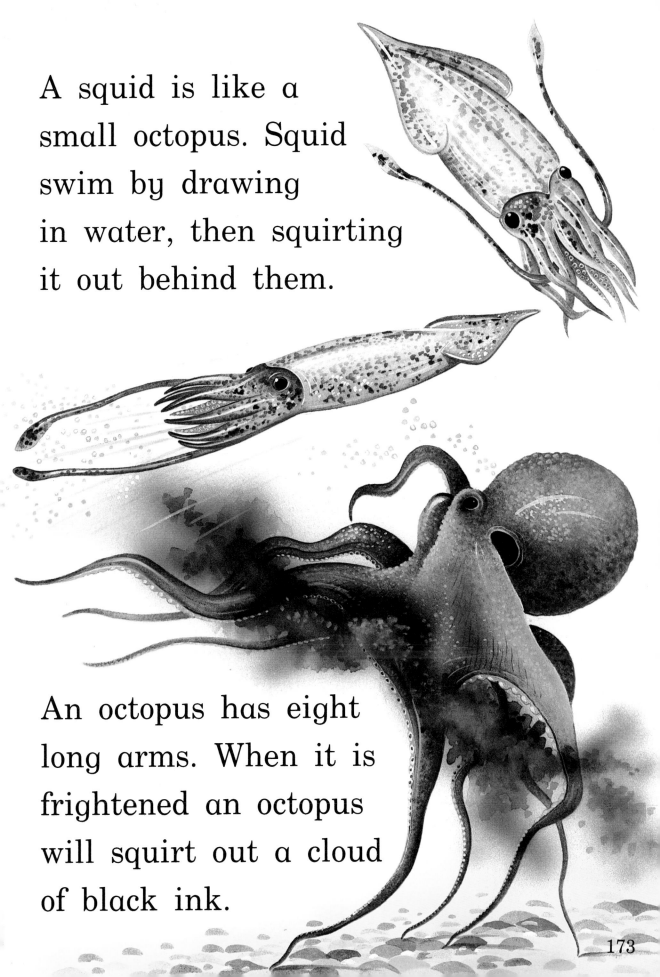

A squid is like a
small octopus. Squid
swim by drawing
in water, then squirting
it out behind them.

An octopus has eight
long arms. When it is
frightened an octopus
will squirt out a cloud
of black ink.

In the very deepest parts of the
sea it is dark and cold. Some very
strange fish live there.
Some of these
fish shine
like lamps in
the dark.

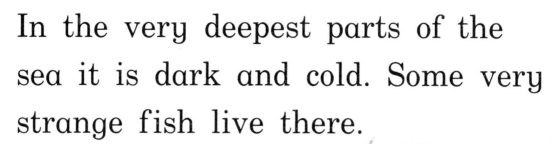

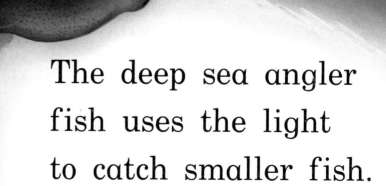

The deep sea angler
fish uses the light
to catch smaller fish.

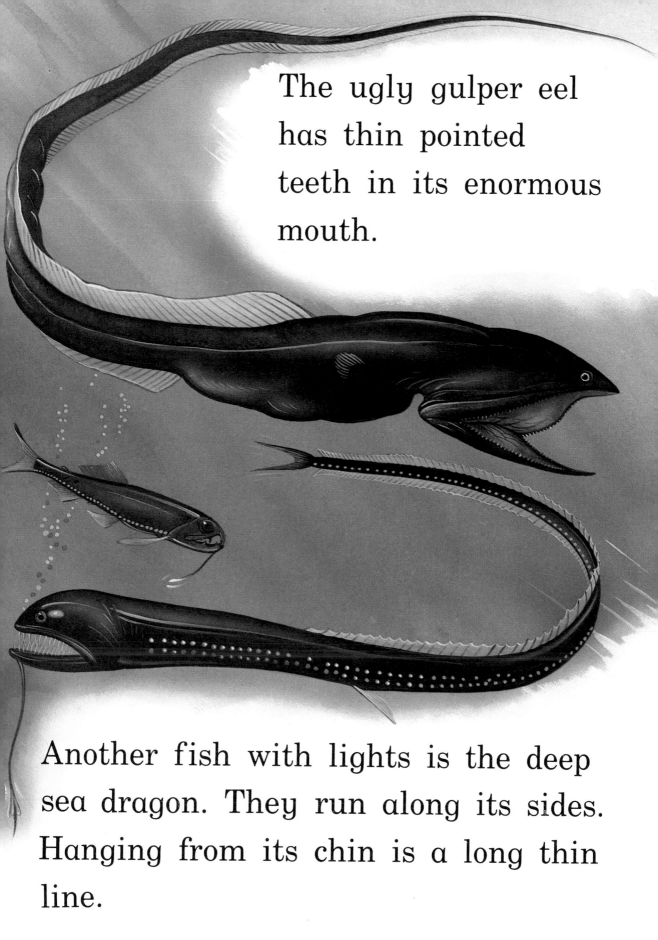

The ugly gulper eel
has thin pointed
teeth in its enormous
mouth.

Another fish with lights is the deep
sea dragon. They run along its sides.
Hanging from its chin is a long thin
line.

With its long nose
the file fish looks
for food between
the rocks. Its skin
is so rough that
carpenters can use
it as sand paper.

The moorish idol fish also has a
long nose. It has strong jaws and
many teeth.

This brightly coloured
fish is called a
butterfly fish.

Another brightly coloured
fish is the angel fish. Just
behind its eyes it has a very
sharp spike. This helps stop
other fish from eating it.

Here is a sun fish.
The sun fish lives
near the surface
of the sea.

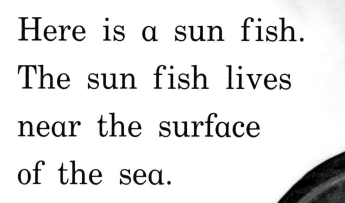

Sea horses do not
look like any other
fish. They cannot
swim very fast. Often
they hang on to
seaweed with their tails.

When flying fish are frightened, they leap from the sea and glide away from their enemies.

If frightened, puffer fish blow themselves up like a prickly balloon. Their sharp spikes stop their enemies from swallowing them.

Brightly coloured tropical fish
can be kept in an aquarium. The
water has to be kept warm. A pump
is used to put fresh air into
the water.

Goldfish can be
kept in an
unheated aquarium.
The plants in
an aquarium help
to keep the
water fresh.

In this book you have read about all these fish. What are their names?

Swordfish

Puffer

Blue Whale

Moorish Idol

Squid

Sea Horse

Electric Ray

Deep Sea Dragon

Angel Fish

File Fish

Sunfish

Gulper Eel

Sailfish

Deep Sea Angler

Flying Fish

Butterfly Fish

Octopus

White Shark

BIRDS

Here is an aviary. Look at all the
pretty birds. David and Julie are
watching them. Birds are the only
animals in the world that have
feathers. A bird has lots of air
inside it. It is like a balloon.

Birds have feathers all over
their bodies. There are big
feathers on the wings. These help
the bird to fly. Small feathers
cover its body. These help the
bird to keep warm.

Look at these small birds.
They flap their wings quickly.
The kingfisher has seen a fish
near the surface. It is diving
very fast. The bird by the flower
is a hummingbird. It hovers in
the air while it feeds. Hummingbirds
can fly backwards.

Some birds are too heavy to leap
into the air. The swans are
running along the water flapping
their wings. Large birds flap
their wings slowly. The bird with
the wide wings is an albatross.
It is floating on the air.

Most birds build nests. Sometimes
they build them in strange places.
The swallow is taking a straw to
its nest inside the barn. Look at
the female pigeon. Her nest is on
a ledge. The robin is building
a nest in an old watering can.

The female bird lays eggs in the
nest. The birds sit on the eggs to
keep them warm. If the eggs get
cold, the baby birds inside them
die. The male bird is feeding
the female. Look in the other nest.
The babies are hatching.

Look at the mother bird with
a fat worm in her beak. The baby
thrushes have their beaks open.
They call loudly. They are always
hungry. Baby thrushes stay in the
nest for two weeks. They leave when
most of their feathers have grown.

Baby geese are called goslings.
They watch their parents to find
out what to eat. They sit on their
mother's back when they are cold
or tired. Look at the goslings.
Young geese take six weeks
to grow all their feathers.

Birds have no teeth. They swallow food without chewing it. Beaks are different shapes because birds eat different kinds of food.

In Australia the kookaburra grabs small snakes behind the head. It batters them against a branch. Look at how the rosella is holding the nut.

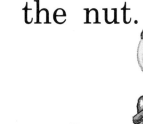

Birds sing and call to each other.
The blackbird is singing to other
blackbirds. He is telling them
"This is where I live, so keep
away". A robin is hopping along
the ground. Look at the birds
splashing about. Some birds love
to have a bath in the dust.

Look at the heron. It is standing on one leg. Its other leg is tucked under its feathers. One of the storks is walking on its toes. What long legs! The other stork is sitting. It is resting. Look at the duck's feet. There is skin between the toes. They use their feet as paddles. They walk on mud without sinking in. A pelican uses its huge beak to scoop fish from the water. The birds with very long, thin beaks are curlews. They eat animals that live deep in the mud. Look at the turnstones. They are turning stones to look for food.

It is night time. The sparrows are
sleeping. Their beaks are tucked
under their wings. When birds
sleep they bend their legs and
their toes lock on to the branch.
This stops them falling off.

The owls are awake. They find
each other in the dark by calling.
They are looking for food. One of
them is swooping down. The little
animal does not see it coming.
Too late!

Birds who hunt and kill other animals are called birds of prey. Eagles, hawks and falcons are all birds of prey. Look at the hawk on the man's glove. The bird swooping away from the water is an osprey. It has a fish in its claws.

The bird of prey in the sky is
a golden eagle. It is looking for
food. It can see a long long way.
The bird with its prey is a kite.
It uses its hooked beak to tear
up its food. Look at the vulture
sitting on the post.

Did you know that some birds do not fly? The ostrich is too heavy to fly. It is the biggest bird in the world. Look at the very large toe on each foot. There is a big claw on the big toe.

Penguins do not fly. They use their wings as flippers.
They move very fast in the sea. They hunt for fish. They jump out of the sea. They use their wings to help them balance.

In this book you have seen lots of birds. You may see some of these birds when you go out.

Robin

Thrush

Pigeon

Chicken

Hawk

Owl

Eagle

Tern

Gull

Petrel

Duck

Goose

Swan